Vegan Recipes in 30 Minutes or Less: Family-Friendly Soup, Salad, Main Dish, Breakfast and Dessert Recipes Inspired by The Mediterranean Diet

by **Vesela Tabakova**
Text copyright(c)2015 Vesela Tabakova

Table Of Contents

Top 80 No-Stress, No-Mess Vegan Dinners – Quick Recipes You Can Make on the Go!

Our fast-paced lives leave us with less and less time for food planning and preparing healthy meals at home. When you don't have a lot of time to spend on dinner and all you want is to relax with your family, these simple and easy to cook vegan dishes will allow you to get a great meal on the table that the whole family will love in an instant.

As a working mother of teenagers with mixed dietary preferences, I don't have the luxury of long periods in the kitchen and am constantly looking for new nutritious and varied vegan meals to add to my everyday menus. Here's a collection of some of my favorite ridiculously quick and easy vegan recipes that take less than half an hour to make and are perfect for a busy weeknight supper or a delicious weekend dinner.

With only about 30 minutes and a couple of your favorite vegetables and legumes, nuts, seeds and superfood aromatic herbs and spices, you can put together an amazing vegan meal that will please everyone at the table and soon become an all time favorite. For me good nutrition is the best gift we can give ourselves and our family members, and the food we prepare at home is just another way of showing love and care for the special people in our lives.

If you want to offer your children a future of well-being and optimum health while at the same time save time in the kitchen - this cookbook is for you!

Salads and Appetizers

Mediterranean Avocado Salad

Serves 5

Prep time: 5 min

Ingredients:

1 avocado, peeled, halved and cut into cubes

1 cup grape tomatoes

1 cup radishes, sliced

2 tbsp drained capers, rinsed

1 large cucumber, quartered and sliced

a handful of rocket leaves

½ cup green olives, pitted, halved

½ cup black olives, pitted, sliced

7-8 fresh basil leaves, torn

2 tbsp olive oil

1 tbsp red wine vinegar

salt and pepper, to taste

Directions:

Place avocado, cucumber, tomatoes, radishes, rocket, olives, capers, and basil in a large salad bowl.

Toss to combine then sprinkle with vinegar and olive oil. Season with salt and pepper, toss again, and serve.

Avocado with Cucumber and Sweet Corn

Serves 5

Prep time: 5 min

Ingredients:

2 avocados, peeled, halved and sliced

2-3 green onions, finely cut

1 cucumber, halved, sliced

1/2 cup canned sweet corn, drained

for the dressing:

2 tbsp olive oil

3 tbsp lemon juice

1 tbsp Dijon mustard

1/2 cup dill, finely cut

salt and pepper, to taste

Directions:

Combine avocados, cucumber and sweet corn in a salad bowl.

Whisk olive oil, lemon juice, dill and mustard until smooth, then drizzle over the salad. Season with salt and pepper to taste, toss to combine, and serve.

Simple Beetroot Salad

Serves 4

Prep time: 25 min

Ingredients:

2-3 small beets, peeled

3 green onions, chopped

3 cloves garlic, pressed

2 tbsp red wine vinegar

2-3 tbsp olive oil

salt, to taste

Directions:

Place the beats in a steam basket set over a pot of boiling water. Steam for about 15-20 minutes or until tender. Set aside to cool.

Grate the beets and put them in a salad bowl. Add the crushed garlic cloves, the finely cut onions and toss to combine. Season with salt, vinegar and olive oil and serve.

Mediterranean Buckwheat Salad

Serves 4-5

Prep time: 10 min

Ingredients:

1 cup buckwheat groats

1 3/4 cups water

1 small red onion, finely chopped

1/2 cucumber, diced

1 cup cherry tomatoes, halved

1 yellow bell pepper, chopped

a bunch of parsley, finely cut

1 preserved lemon, finely chopped

1 cup chickpeas, cooked or canned, drained

juice of half lemon

1 tsp dried basil

2 tbsp olive oil

salt and black pepper, to taste

Directions:

Heat a large, dry saucepan and toast the buckwheat for about three minutes. Boil the water and add it carefully to the buckwheat. Cover, reduce heat and simmer until buckwheat is tender and all liquid is absorbed (5-7 minutes). Remove from heat, fluff with a fork and set aside to cool.

Mix the buckwheat with the chopped onion, bell pepper, cucumber, cherry tomatoes, parsley, preserved lemon and chickpeas in a salad bowl.

Whisk the lemon juice, olive oil and basil, season with salt and pepper to taste, then pour over the salad and stir. Serve at room temperature.

Spicy Buckwheat Vegetable Salad

Serves 4-5

Prep time: 15 min

Ingredients:

1 cup buckwheat groats

2 cups vegetable broth

2 tomatoes, diced

1/2 cup green onions, chopped

1/2 cup parsley leaves, finely chopped

1/2 cup fresh mint leaves, very finely chopped

1/2 yellow bell pepper, chopped

1 cucumber, peeled and cut into 1/4-inch cubes

1/2 cup cooked or canned brown lentils, drained

1/4 cup freshly squeezed lemon juice

1 tsp chili sauce

Directions:

Heat a large, dry saucepan and toast the buckwheat for about 3 minutes. Boil the vegetable broth and add it carefully to the buckwheat. Cover, reduce heat and simmer until buckwheat is tender and all liquid is absorbed (5-7 minutes). Remove from heat, fluff with a fork and set aside to cool.

Chop all vegetables and add them together with the lentils to the buckwheat. Mix the lemon juice and remaining ingredients well and drizzle over the buckwheat mixture. Stir well to distribute the dressing evenly.

Buckwheat Salad with Asparagus and Roasted Peppers

Serves 4-5

Prep time: 15 min

Ingredients:

1 cup buckwheat groats

1 3/4 cups vegetable broth

1/2 lb asparagus, trimmed and cut into 1 inch pieces

4 roasted red bell peppers, peeled and diced

2-3 green onions, finely chopped

2 garlic cloves, crushed

1 tbsp red wine vinegar

3 tbsp olive oil

1/2 cup fresh parsley leaves, finely cut

Directions:

Heat a large dry saucepan and toast the buckwheat for about 3 minutes. Boil the vegetable broth and add it carefully to the buckwheat. Cover, reduce heat and simmer until buckwheat is tender and all liquid is absorbed (5-7 minutes). Remove from heat, fluff with a fork and set aside to cool.

Rinse out the saucepan and bring about an inch of water to a boil. Cook the asparagus in a steamer basket or colander, 2-3 minutes until tender. Transfer the asparagus in a large bowl along with the roasted peppers. Add in the green onions, garlic, red wine vinegar, salt, pepper and olive oil. Stir to combine. Add the buckwheat to the vegetable mixture. Sprinkle with parsley and toss the salad gently. Serve at room temperature.

Greek Chickpea Salad

Serves 4

Prep time: 10 min

Ingredients:

1 cup canned chickpeas, drained and rinsed

3-4 green onions, finely cut

1 small cucumber, peeled and diced

2 green bell peppers, diced

2 tomatoes, diced

2 tsp chopped fresh parsley

1 cup black olives, pitted

1 tsp capers, drained and rinsed

juice of 1/2 a lemon

1 tbsp olive oil

1 tsp balsamic vinegar

salt and pepper, to taste

a pinch of dried oregano

Directions:

In a medium bowl, toss together the chickpeas, green onions, cucumber, bell pepper, tomato, parsley, olives, capers, and lemon juice.

In a smaller bowl, stir together the remaining ingredients and pour over the chickpea salad. Toss well to coat and serve.

Quinoa and Black Bean Salad

Serves 6

Prep time: 25 min

Ingredients:

1 cup quinoa

2 cups water

1 cup black beans, cooked, rinsed and drained

1/2 cup sweet corn, cooked

1 red bell pepper, deseeded and chopped

4 green onions, chopped

1 garlic clove, crushed

1 tbsp dry mint

2 tbsp lemon juice

1/2 tsp salt

1 tbsp apple cider vinegar

4 tbsp olive oil

Directions:

Rinse quinoa in a fine sieve under cold running water until the water runs clear. Put quinoa in a pot with two cups of water. Bring to a boil, then reduce heat, cover and simmer for 15 minutes or until the water is absorbed and quinoa is tender. Fluff quinoa with a fork and set aside to cool.

Put beans, corn, bell pepper, green onions and garlic in a bowl and toss with vinegar and black pepper to taste. Add quinoa and toss well again.

In a separate bowl whisk together lemon juice, salt and olive oil and drizzle over the salad. Toss well and serve.

Fried Zucchinis with Tomato Sauce

Serves 4

Prep time: 30 min

Ingredients:

4 zucchinis medium size

1 cup flour

Salt

For the tomato sauce

4-5 ripe tomatoes, skinned and grated

1 carrot

½ onion

2 cloves garlic, whole

1 tsp salt

11/2 cup sunflower oil

1 tsp sugar

3.5 oz flour

1/2 cup parsley, finely cut

Directions:

Wash and peel the zucchinis, and cut them in thin diagonal slices or in rings. Sprinkle with salt and leave aside in a suitable bowl placing it inclined to drain away the juices.

Coat the zucchinis with flour, then fry turning on both sides until they are golden-brown (about 3 minutes on each side). Transfer to paper towels and pat dry.

Heat the oil in a large skillet and cook the onion and until soft. Add the grated tomatoes together with two whole garlic cloves.

Season with salt and a teaspoon of sugar. Simmer at low heat until thick and ready. Sprinkle with parsley and pour over the fried zucchinis.

Brown Lentil Salad

Serves 4

Prep time: 5 min

Ingredients:

1 can lentils, drained and rinsed

1 red onion, thinly sliced

1 tomato, diced

1 red bell pepper, chopped

2 garlic cloves, crushed

2 tbsp lemon juice

salt and pepper, to taste

1/3 cup parsley leaves, finely cut, to serve

Directions:

Place lentils, red onion, tomato, bell pepper, and lemon juice in a large bowl. Season with salt and black pepper to taste.

Toss to combine, sprinkle with parsley, and serve.

Green Salad

Serves 4

Prep time: 10 min

Ingredients:

1 head of lettuce, cut in strips

1 cucumber, peeled and cut

8-9 radishes, cut

4-5 green onions

1/2 cup canned sweet corn

the juice of half a lemon or 2 tbsp of white wine vinegar

3 tbsp sunflower or olive oil

salt, to taste

Directions:

Cut the lettuce into thin strips. Slice the cucumber and the radishes as thinly as possible and chop the green onions.

Combine the vegetables in a large salad bowl; add the lemon juice and oil and season with salt to taste.

Beet and Bean Sprout Salad

Serves 4

Prep time: 10 min

Ingredients:

7 beet greens, finely sliced

2 medium tomatoes, sliced

1 cup bean sprouts, washed

1 tbsp grated lemon rind

2 garlic cloves, crushed

1/4 cup lemon juice

1/4 cup olive oil

1 tsp salt

Directions:

In a large bowl, toss together the beet greens, bean sprouts and tomatoes.

Combine oil and lemon juice with lemon rind, salt and garlic and pour over the salad. Serve chilled.

Cabbage Salad

Serves 4

Prep time: 10 min

Ingredients:

9 oz fresh white cabbage, shredded

9 oz carrots, shredded

9 oz white turnips, shredded

½ cup parsley, finely cut

2 tbsp white vinegar

3 tbsp olive oil

salt, to taste

Directions:

Combine first three ingredients in a large bowl - and mix well. Add the salt, vinegar and oil. Stir, and sprinkle with parsley.

Roasted Peppers with Garlic and Parsley

Serves 4-6

Prep time: 30 min

Ingredients:

2 lb red and green bell peppers

1/2 cup sunflower oil

5-6 tbsp white vinegar

3-4 cloves garlic, chopped

1 cup parsley, finely cut

salt and pepper, to taste

Directions:

Grill the peppers or roast them in the oven at 400 F until the skins are a little burnt. Place the roasted peppers in a brown paper bag or a lidded container and leave covered for about 10 minutes. This makes it easier to peel them. Peel the skins and remove the seeds.

Cut the peppers into strips lengthwise and layer them in a bowl. Mix together the oil, vinegar, salt and pepper, chopped garlic and the chopped parsley leaves. Pour over the peppers.

Simple Cucumber Salad

Serves 4

Prep time: 5 min

Ingredients:

2 medium cucumbers, peeled and sliced

a bunch of fresh dill, finely cut

2 cloves garlic, crushed

3 tbsp white wine vinegar

3 tbsp olive oil

salt, to taste

Directions:

Cut the cucumbers in rings and put them in a salad bowl. Add in dill, garlic, salt, vinegar and oil.

Toss to combine and serve.

Baby Spinach Salad

Serves 4

Prep time: 5 min

Ingredients:

1 bag baby spinach, washed and dried

1 red bell pepper, cut in slices

1 cup cherry tomatoes, cut in halves

1 red onion, finely chopped

1 cup black olives, pitted

1 tsp dried oregano

1 large garlic clove

3 tbsp red wine vinegar

4 tbsp olive oil

salt and freshly ground black pepper, to taste

Directions:

Prepare the dressing by blending the garlic and the oregano with the olive oil and the vinegar in a food processor.

Place the spinach leaves in a large salad bowl and toss with the dressing. Add the rest of the ingredients and give everything a toss again.

Season to taste with black pepper and salt.

Kale Salad with Creamy Tahini Dressing

Serves 4

Prep time: 5 min

Ingredients:

1 head kale

2 cucumbers, peeled and diced

1 avocado, peeled and diced

1 red onion, finely chopped

1 cup cherry tomatoes, halved

for the dressing

1/3 cup tahini

1/2 cup water

2 garlic cloves, minsed

3 tbsp lemon juice

4 tbsp olive oil

salt and freshly ground black pepper, to taste

Directions:

Prepare the dressing by whisking all ingredients.

Place all salad ingredients in bowl and toss with the dressing.

Season to taste with black pepper and salt.

Tabbouleh

Serves 6

Prep time: 20 min

Ingredients:

1 cup raw bulgur

2 cups boiling water

a bunch of parsley, finely cut

2 tomatoes, chopped

3 tbsp olive oil

2 garlic cloves, minced

6-7 fresh onions, chopped

1 tbsp fresh mint leaves, chopped

juice of two lemons

salt and black pepper, to taste

Directions:

Bring water and salt to a boil, then pour over bulgur. Cover and set aside for 15 minutes to steam. Drain excess water and fluff with a fork.

In a large bowl, mix together the parsley, tomatoes, olive oil, garlic, green onions and mint. Stir in the chilled bulgur and season to taste with salt, pepper and lemon juice.

Fatoush

Serves 6

Prep time: 10 min

Ingredients:

2 cups lettuce, washed, dried, and chopped

2 tomatoes, diced

1 cucumber, peeled and chopped

1 green pepper, seeded and chopped

1 cup radishes, sliced

1 small red onion, finely chopped

1 cup parsley, finely cut

2 tbsp finely chopped fresh mint

3 tbsp olive oil

4 tbsp lemon juice

salt and black pepper, to taste

2 whole-wheat pita breads

Directions:

Toast the pita breads in a skillet until they are browned and crisp. Set aside.

Place the lettuce, tomatoes, cucumbers, green pepper, radishes, onion, parsley and mint in a salad bowl. Break up the toasted pita into bite-size pieces and add to the salad.

Make the dressing by whisking together the olive oil with the lemon juice, a pinch of salt and some black pepper. Toss together until everything is coated with the dressing and serve.

Chickpea and Avocado Dip

Serves: 4

Prep time: 2-3 min

Ingredients:

1 can chickpeas, drained

1 ripe avocado, peeled and chopped

3 tbsp tahini

1/2 cup lemon juice

2 garlic cloves, crushed

4 tbsp finely cut parsley

1 tbsp olive oil

1/2 tsp cumin

salt and pepper, to taste

Directions:

Heat olive oil in a skillet pan over medium-high heat. Cook half the chickpeas, stirring, for 3-4 minutes or until golden. Set aside to cool.

Blend remaining chickpeas with avocado, tahini, lemon juice, garlic and cumin until smooth.

Season with salt and pepper and spoon into a serving bowl. Top with chickpeas, sprinkle with parsley and serve.

Zucchini and Avocado Dip

Serves: 4

Prep time: 5 min

Ingredients:

1 large zucchini, peeled and diced

1 ripe avocado, peeled and chopped

3 garlic cloves, chopped

2 tbsp tahini

3 tbsp olive oil

1/4 cup lemon juice

2 tbsp dill, finely cut

salt, to taste

Directions:

Combine all ingredients in a blender and pulse until smooth.

Rocket and Cashew Spread

Serves: 4

Prep time: 30 min

Ingredients:

1 1/2 cup cashews

¼ cup nutritional yeast

2 garlic cloves, chopped

3 cups rocket leaves

5 tbsp olive oil

3 tbsp lemon juice

2 tbsp dill, finely cut

salt, to taste

Directions:

Combine the cashews, nutritional yeast and garlic in a blender and pulse until the ingredients are mixed but the cashews are still chunky. Set aside in a bowl.

Add in the olive oil and lemon juice first, and then the rocket. Pulse to blend well.

Mix rocket mixture into cashew mixture, and season with salt and pepper to taste.

Turkish Spinach Salad

Serves 1-2

Prep time: 5-6 min

Ingredients:

about 8-9 spinach stems

water to boil the stems

1-2 garlic cloves, crushed

lemon juice or vinegar, to taste

4 tbsp olive oil

salt, to taste

Directions:

Trim the stems so that they remain whole. Wash them very well. Steam the spinach stems in a basket over boiling water for 2-3 minutes or until wilted but not too fluffy.

Place the spinach stems on a plate and sprinkle with crushed garlic, olive oil, lemon juice and salt.

Soups

Spiced Root Soup

Serves 4

Prep time: 30 min

Ingredients:

2 parsnips, peeled, chopped

2 leeks, chopped

2 carrots, chopped

1 potato, peeled and diced

4 cups vegetable broth

1/2 cup almond milk

1 garlic clove

3 tbsp olive oil

1 tbsp curry powder

1/2 tsp cumin

salt and freshly ground pepper, to taste

Directions:

Heat olive oil in a large saucepan and sauté the leeks and garlic together with the curry powder and cumin. Stir in the parsnips, carrot and potato and cook, stirring often, for 10 minutes.

Add the vegetable broth, bring to the boil, and simmer for 20 minutes, or until the vegetables are tender.

Set aside to cool then blend in batches until smooth. Return soup to pan over low heat and stir in the almond milk. Season with salt and black pepper to taste.

Creamy Red Lentil Soup

Serves: 4

Prep time: 30 min

Ingredients:

1 cup red lentils

1/2 small onion, chopped

1 garlic clove, chopped

1 red pepper, chopped

3 cups water

1 can coconut milk

3 tbsp olive oil

1 tsp paprika

1/2 tsp ginger

salt and black pepper, to taste

Directions:

Heat olive oil in a large saucepan and sauté onion, garlic, red pepper, paprika, ginger and cumin, stirring.

Add in red lentils and water. Bring to a boil, cover, and simmer for 20 minutes. Add in coconut milk and simmer for 5 more minutes.

Remove from heat, season with salt and black pepper, and blend until smooth.

Lentil, Quinoa and Kale Soup

Serves: 4

Prep time: 30 min

Ingredients:

2 medium leeks, chopped

2 garlic cloves, chopped

2 bay leaves

1 can tomatoes, diced and undrained

1/2 cup red lentils

1/2 cup quinoa

1 bunch kale, coarsely chopped

4 cups vegetable broth

3 tbsp olive oil

1 tbsp paprika

½ tsp cumin

Directions:

Heat olive oil in a large saucepan over medium-high heat and sauté leeks and garlic until fragrant.

Add in cumin, paprika, tomatoes, lentils, quinoa and vegetable broth. Season with salt and pepper.

Cover and bring to a boil then reduce heat and simmer for 20 minutes. Add in kale and let it simmer for a few minutes more until it wilts.

Spinach and Mushroom Soup

Serves: 4-5

Prep time: 30 min

Ingredients:

1 small onion, finely cut

1 small carrot, chopped

1 small zucchini, diced

1 medium potato, diced

6-7 white button mushrooms, chopped

2 cups chopped fresh spinach

4 cups vegetable broth or water

4 tbsp olive oil

salt and black pepper, to taste

Directions:

Heat olive oil in a large pot over medium heat. Add in potato, onion and mushroom and cook until vegetables are soft but not mushy.

Add the chopped fresh spinach, zucchini and vegetable broth, and simmer for about 20 minutes. Season to taste with salt and pepper.

Tomato Soup

Serves: 5-6

Prep time: 30 min

Ingredients:

4 cups chopped fresh tomatoes or 28 oz can tomatoes

1/3 cup rice

3 cups water

1 large onion, diced

4 garlic cloves, minced

3 tbsp olive oil

1 tbsp paprika

1 tsp salt

1 tsp sugar

½ cup fresh parsley, finely cut, to serve

Directions:

Heat olive oil in a large pot over medium heat and gently sauté the onions and garlic in olive oil. When the onions have softened, add in paprika, tomatoes and water.

Bring to a boil, add in rice, lower heat and simmer for 20 minutes.

Blend the soup, then return to the pot, add a teaspoon of sugar, and bring to the boil again.

Simmer for 5 minutes stirring occasionally. Sprinkle with parsley and serve.

Moroccan Lentil Soup

Serves 6-7

Prep time: 30 min

Ingredients:

1 cup red lentils

1/2 cup canned chickpeas, drained

1 onion, chopped

2 cloves garlic, minced

1 cup canned tomatoes, chopped

1/2 cup canned white beans, drained

3 carrots, diced

1 celery rib, diced

5 cups water

1 tsp ginger, grated

1 tsp ground cardamom

1/2 tsp cumin

3 tbsp olive oil

salt, to taste

Directions:

In a large pot, sauté onion, garlic and ginger in olive oil for about 3-4 minutes. Add the water, lentils, chickpeas, white beans, tomatoes, carrots, celery, cardamom and cumin.

Bring to a boil and simmer for 25 minutes or until the lentils are tender. Season with salt to taste. Puree half the soup in a food processor or blender. Return the pureed soup to the pot, stir, and serve.

Italian Vegetable Soup

Serves 4-5

Prep time: 30 min

Ingredients:

¼ cabbage, chopped

2 carrots, chopped

1 celery rib, thinly sliced

1 small onion, chopped

2 garlic cloves, chopped

2 tbsp olive oil

3 cups water

1 cup canned tomatoes, diced, undrained

1 cup fresh spinach, torn

1/2 cup pasta, cooked

black pepper and salt, to taste

Directions:

Sauté the carrots, cabbage, celery, onion and garlic in oil for 5 minutes in a deep saucepan.

Add in water, tomatoes and bring to a boil. Reduce heat and simmer uncovered, for 20 minutes, or until all vegetables are tender.

Stir in spinach and pasta, and season with pepper and salt to taste.

Creamy Zucchini Soup

Serves 4

Prep time: 25 min

Ingredients:

5 zucchinis, peeled, thinly sliced

1 onion, finely chopped

2 garlic cloves, crushed

1 large potato, peeled and chopped

4 cups vegetable broth

1/4 cup fresh basil leaves

1 tsp sugar

salt and pepper, to taste

Directions:

Heat oil in a saucepan over medium heat and sauté the onion and garlic, stirring, for 2-3 minutes or until soft.

Add vegetable broth and bring to the boil, then reduce heat to medium-low. Add in zucchinis, the potato, a teaspoon of sugar and simmer, stirring occasionally, for 15 minutes, or until the zucchinis are tender.

Add in basil and simmer for 2-3 minutes. Set aside to cool then blend in batches and reheat.

Garden Vegetable Soup

Serves 6

Prep time: 25 min

Ingredients:

1 small onion, finely cut

1 zucchini, peeled and diced

2 cups Brussels sprouts

1 large carrot, chopped

2 garlic cloves, cut

4 cups vegetable broth

1 tomato, diced

1/4 cup chopped celery leaves

3 tbsp olive oil

salt, to taste

black pepper, to taste

Directions:

In a deep soup pot, gently sauté the onion, zucchini, Brussels sprouts, carrot and garlic for about 5 minutes. Add in vegetable broth and tomato and bring to the boil.

Season with salt and black pepper to taste and simmer for 10 minutes or until the vegetables are tender but still holding their shape. Stir in the celery leaves.

Cover again and simmer for a further 5 minutes.

Beetroot and Carrot Soup

Serves 4

Prep time: 30 min

Ingredients:

4 beets, washed, peeled and diced

3 carrots, peeled, chopped

2 potatoes, peeled and chopped

2 cups vegetable broth

2 cups water

2 tbsp olive oil

3-4 green onions, finely cut, to serve

Directions:

Heat olive oil in a saucepan over medium-high heat and sauté the onion and carrots until tender. Add in beets, potatoes, vegetable broth and water.

Bring to the boil, reduce heat to medium and simmer, partially covered, for 20 minutes, or until the beets are tender. Cool slightly.

Blend soup in batches until smooth. Return it to pan over low heat and cook, stirring, for 2-3 minutes, or until heated through. Season with salt and pepper. Serve sprinkled with green onions.

Creamy Celery Soup

Serves: 4

Prep time: 30 min

Ingredients:

2 cups chopped celery ribs or celeriac

1 potato, peeled and diced

1/2 small onion, chopped

1 garlic clove, crushed

3 cups vegetable broth

1 cup almond milk

1 tbsp fresh dill, finely cut

3 tbsp olive oil

salt and black pepper, to taste

Directions:

Heat olive oil over medium-high heat and sauté onion, garlic, celery and potato for 3-4 minutes, stirring. Add in vegetable broth.

Bring to a boil then reduce heat and simmer, covered, for 20 minutes. Stir in the almond milk and dill and blend until smooth.

Return soup to the pot and cook over medium-high heat until heated through. Season with salt and black pepper to taste and serve.

Creamy Cauliflower Soup

Serves 5-6

Prep time: 30 min

Ingredients:

1 medium head cauliflower, chopped

1 large onion, finely cut

2-3 garlic cloves, minced

3 cups vegetable broth

¼ cup olive oil

salt, to taste

fresh ground black pepper, to taste

Directions:

Heat the olive oil in a large pot over medium heat and gently sauté the onion, cauliflower and garlic. Stir in the vegetable broth and bring the mixture to a boil.

Reduce heat, cover, and simmer for 20 minutes. Remove the soup from heat and blend in a blender or with a hand mixer. Season with salt and pepper.

Pumpkin and Bell Pepper Soup

Serves 4

Prep time: 30 min

Ingredients:

2 medium leeks, chopped

2 cups diced pumpkin

2 red peppers, cut into small pieces

1 can tomatoes, undrained, crushed

3 cups vegetable broth

1/2 tsp cumin

salt and black pepper, to taste

Directions:

Heat the olive oil in a medium saucepan and gently sauté the leek for 2-3 minutes. Add the pumpkin and bell peppers and cook, stirring, for 5 minutes. Add in tomatoes, broth, and cumin and bring to the boil.

Cover, reduce heat to low and simmer, stirring occasionally, for 20 minutes or until the vegetables are tender. Season with salt and pepper and leave aside to cool. Blend in batches and re-heat to serve.

Cold Avocado Soup

Serves 6-7

Prep time: 5 min

Ingredients:

2 ripe avocados, peeled and chopped

3 tomatoes, peeled and diced

1/2 small onion, sliced

1 green pepper, sliced

1 small cucumber, peeled and sliced

salt, to taste

4 tbsp olive oil

1 tbsp apple vinegar

fresh parsley leaves, finely cut, to serve

Directions:

Place the avocados, tomatoes, onion, green pepper, cucumber, salt, olive oil and vinegar in a blender or food processor.

Puree until smooth, adding small amounts of cold water, if needed, to achieve desired consistency. Serve the soup chilled.

Creamy Asparagus Soup

Serves: 4

Prep time: 30 min

Ingredients:

1 lb fresh asparagus, cut into pieces

1 small onion, chopped

3 garlic cloves, chopped

½ cup raw cashews, soaked in warm water for 1 hour

4 cups vegetable broth

2 tbsp olive oil

lemon juice, to taste

Directions:

Sauté the onion for 3-4 minutes, stirring. Add in garlic and sauté for a minute more. Add in asparagus and sauté for 3-4 minutes.

Add broth, season with salt and pepper and bring to a boil then reduce heat and simmer for 20 minutes.

Set aside to cool, add cashews, and blend, until smooth. Season with lemon juice and serve.

Main Dishes

Hearty Lentil and Spinach Spaghetti

Serves: 4-5

Prep time: 30 min

Ingredients:

12 oz whole wheat spaghetti

1 small onion, very finely cut

1 can brown lentils, rinsed and drained

1/2 cup black olives, pitted and halved

2 garlic cloves, chopped

2 cups tomato sauce

2 cups water

1 cup fresh spinach leaves, chopped

3 tbsp olive oil

1 tbsp summer savory

1 tsp salt

Directions:

In a deep saucepan over medium-high heat, heat olive oil. Gently sauté the onion, garlic, lentils, olives, water and tomato sauce.

Bring to a boil and add in spaghetti and summer savory. Reduce heat and simmer until the spaghetti is cooked to al dente.

Add spinach and cook for 1-2 minutes or until it wilts.

Avocado and Rocket Pasta

Serves: 4

Prep time: 15 min

Ingredients:

3 cups cooked small pasta

½ cup cooked sweet corn

1 large avocado, peeled and diced

1 cup baby rocket leaves

5-6 fresh basil leaves, chopped

3 tbsp olive oil

3 tbsp lemon juice

Directions:

Whisk olive oil, lemon juice and basil in a small bowl. Season with salt and pepper to taste.

Combine pasta, avocado, corn and baby rocket. Add oil mixture and toss to combine.

Delicious Broccoli Pasta

Serves: 4

Prep time: 15 min

Ingredients:

3 cups cooked small pasta

2 cups broccoli florets, boiled

1/3 cup walnuts, chopped

2 garlic cloves, chopped

10 cherry tomatoes, halved

5-6 fresh basil leaves

3 tbsp olive oil

3 tbsp lemon juice

Directions:

Place broccoli in a pan of boiling water and cook the florets for 6-8 minutes.

Combine olive oil, lemon juice, garlic, walnuts, basil and broccoli in a blender. Season with salt and pepper to taste and blend until smooth.

Combine pasta, broccoli mixture and cherry tomatoes, toss, and serve.

One-pot Artichoke Spaghetti

Serves: 4-5

Prep time: 30 min

Ingredients:

12 oz whole wheat spaghetti

1 small onion, very finely cut

1 can artichoke hearts, rinsed, drained, and chopped

1/2 cup black olives, pitted and halved

2 garlic cloves, chopped

2 cups tomato sauce

2 cups water

1 cup fresh spinach leaves, chopped

3 tbsp olive oil

1 tsp dried basil

1 tsp dried oregano

1/2 tsp black pepper

1 tsp salt

Directions:

In a deep saucepan over medium-high heat, heat olive oil. Gently sauté the onion and garlic. Add in olives, artichoke hearts, tomato sauce, water, and spices.

Bring to a boil and stir in spaghetti. Reduce heat and simmer until the spaghetti is cooked to al dente.

Creamy Garlic Pasta with Sun-dried Tomatoes and Rocket

Serves: 4-5

Prep time: 30 min

Ingredients:

12 oz whole wheat pasta

1/2 onion, very finely cut

1 cup sun-dried tomatoes

1/2 cup black olives, pitted and halved

7-8 garlic cloves, chopped

2-3 tbsp all purpose flour

2.5 cups unsweetened almond milk

a bunch of baby rocket leaves

3 tbsp olive oil

1 tsp dried basil

1/2 tsp black pepper

1 tsp salt

Directions:

Bring a large pot of water to a boil and cook pasta according to package instructions. When done, drain, cover and set aside.

In a deep saucepan over medium-high heat, heat olive oil. Gently sauté the onion and garlic for 1-2 minutes, until fragrant. Stir in flour and mix with a whisk. Slowly whisk in the almond milk a little at a time so clumps don't form.

Season with salt and black pepper and bring to a simmer. Cook for about 4-5 minutes to thicken.

Once the sauce has reached desired thickness, adjust seasonings as needed. Add pasta, sun-dried tomatoes and and rocket and stir.

Creamy Mushroom Pasta

Serves: 4-5

Prep time: 30 min

Ingredients:

12 oz whole wheat penne

1/2 onion, very finely cut

10-15 white button mushrooms, sliced

3-4 garlic cloves, chopped

2-3 tbsp all purpose flour

2.5 cups unsweetened almond milk

3 tbsp olive oil

1 tsp dried thyme

1 tsp dried sage

1 tsp salt

1 cup fresh parsley, finely cut, to serve

3 tablespoons blanched sliced almonds, to serve

Directions:

Bring a large pot of water to a boil and cook pasta according to package instructions. When done, drain, cover and set aside.

Meanwhile, in a deep saucepan over medium-high heat, heat olive oil. Gently sauté the onion and garlic for 1-2 minutes, until fragrant. Stir in the mushrooms, thyme and sage and cook, stirring, for 5-6 minutes. Add in flour and mix with a whisk.

Slowly whisk in the almond milk a little at a time so clumps don't form. Season with salt and black pepper and bring to a simmer.

Cook for about 5 minutes to thicken.

Once the sauce has reached desired thickness, adjust seasonings as needed. Add in pasta, parsley and almonds, stir, and serve.

Creamy Avocado Pasta

Serves: 4

Prep time: 30 min

Ingredients:

12 oz whole wheat pasta

½ cup canned chickpeas

2 ripe avocados, peeled and diced

2 garlic cloves, chopped

1 cup cherry tomatoes, halved

5-6 fresh basil leaves, chopped

3 tbsp olive oil

3 tbsp lemon juice

Directions:

In a large pot of boiling salted water, cook pasta according to package instructions; drain well.

Combine avocados, basil, garlic and lemon juice in a food processor and season with salt and pepper to taste.

With the motor running, add olive oil in a slow stream until emulsified; set aside.

Combine pasta, avocado sauce, cherry tomatoes and chickpeas. Serve immediately.

Peanut and Vegetable Pasta

Serves: 4

Prep time: 30 min

Ingredients:

12 oz whole wheat pasta

5-6 white button mushrooms

2 red peppers, cut

1 eggplant, peeled and diced

4-5 green onions, finely cut

2 garlic cloves, chopped

3 tbsp sesame seeds

1/2 cup peanuts, crushed

1/2 tsp dried oregano

salt and black pepper, to taste

Directions:

In a large pot of boiling salted water, cook pasta according to package instructions; drain well.

In a deep saucepan over medium-high heat, heat olive oil. Gently sauté the onions, garlic, peanuts and sesame seeds.

Add in mushrooms, eggplant and peppers. Simmer for 5-6 minutes, stirring from time to time.

Combine pasta and vegetable sauce and serve.

Baked Falafels

Serves: 7

Prep time: 20-30 min

Ingredients:

1 can chickpeas, drained and rinsed

1 small carrot, chopped

1 small onion, chopped

3 garlic cloves, minced

½ cup fresh parsley, finely cut

¼ cup whole wheat flour

¼ cup tahini

4 tbsp olive oil

2-3 tbsp lemon juice

2 tsp cumin (or to taste)

1 tsp salt

black pepper, to taste

Directions:

Combine the carrots, chickpeas, onion and garlic in a food processor and blend until smooth. Add in parsley and the remaining ingredients.

Using a large tablespoon form batter into burgers. Bake, in a preheated to 375 F oven, until golden.

Turkish Eggplant and Chickpea Stew

Serves 4

Prep time: 30 min

Ingredients:

2-3 eggplants, peeled and diced

1 onion, chopped

2-3 garlic cloves, crushed

1 can chickpeas, drained

1 can tomatoes, undrained, diced

1 tbsp paprika

1/2 tsp cinnamon

1 tsp cumin

3 tbsp olive oil

salt and pepper, to taste

Directions:

Heat olive oil in a large, deep frying pan and sauté the onions and crushed garlic.

Add paprika, cumin and cinnamon. Stir well to coat evenly. Sauté for 3-4 minutes or until the onions have softened.

Add the eggplant, tomatoes and chickpeas. Bring to a boil, lower heat, and simmer, covered, for 15 minutes, or until the eggplant is tender. Uncover and simmer for a few more minutes or until the liquid evaporates.

Green Pea and Mushroom Stew

Serves 4

Prep time: 30 min

Ingredients:

1 bag frozen green peas

1 large carrot, cut

4 large white button mushrooms, sliced

1 onion, finely cut

2-3 garlic cloves, finely cut

4 tbsp olive oil

1 tbsp paprika

1/2 cup water

1/2 cup finely chopped dill, to serve

Directions:

In a saucepan, sauté the mushrooms, onion, carrot and garlic for 3-4 minutes, stirring. Add in paprika and the green peas and stir to combine.

Bring to a boil and simmer for about 20 minutes. When ready, sprinkle with dill, and serve.

Potato and Leek Stew

Serves 4

Prep time: 30 min

Ingredients:

2-3 large potatoes, peeled and diced

3-4 leeks cut into thick rings

5-6 tbsp olive oil

1 tsp paprika

salt, to taste

1/2 cup parsley, finely cut

Directions:

Put the potatoes and the leeks in a pot along with the olive oil, paprika and some water. The water should cover the vegetables.

Season with salt and bring to a boil then simmer for 30 minutes or until the vegetables are tender. Sprinkle with parsley and serve.

Zucchinis with Chickpeas and Rice

Serves 4

Prep time: 30 min

Ingredients:

3 zucchinis, peeled and diced

1 bunch green onions, finely chopped

2 medium tomatoes, diced

1/2 can chickpeas, drained

1/2 cup rice

1/2 cup black olives, pitted and halved

2 cups water

5 tbsp sunflower oil

1 tsp salt

1 tsp paprika

1 tsp black pepper

1/2 cup fresh dill, finely cut

Directions:

Sauté the onions in olive oil and a little water for 1-2 minutes or until soft.

Transfer the onions in a baking dish and add in zucchinis, chickpeas, tomatoes, olives, rice, salt, paprika, black pepper and water. Stir to combine well.

Cover with a lid or aluminum foil and bake at 350 F for 20 minutes, or until the rice is done. Sprinkle with dill and serve.

Spinach with Rice

Serves 4

Prep time: 30 min

Ingredients:

1.5 lb fresh spinach, washed, drained and chopped

1/2 cup rice

1 onion, finely cut

1 carrot, cut

4 tbsp olive oil

2 cups water

salt and black pepper, to taste

Directions:

Heat the oil in a large skillet and cook the onions and carrot until tender. Add in paprika and the washed and drained rice and stir to combine.

Add two cups of warm water, stirring constantly as the rice absorbs it, and simmer for 10 more minutes.

Add spinach and simmer for 5 minutes or until it wilts. Season with salt and black pepper to taste and serve.

Vegetable Stew

Serves 4-5

Prep time: 30 min

Ingredients:

2-3 potatoes, peeled and diced

1-2 tomatoes, diced

1-2 carrots, chopped

1 onion, finely chopped

2 garlic cloves, chopped

1 zucchini, peeled and diced

1 eggplant, peeled and diced

1 celery rib, chopped

1/2 cup green peas, frozen

1/2 bag frozen green beans

1/2 cup water

4 tbsp olive oil

1 tsp paprika

1 tsp salt

1 cup fresh parsley, finely cut, to serve

Directions:

In a deep casserole, gently sauté the finely chopped onion, carrots, garlic and celery in olive oil.

Add in green peas, green beans, paprika and salt and stir to combine. Pour over 1/2 cup of water and remaining vegetables and cook for about 20 minutes or until vegetables are tender. Sprinkle with fresh parsley and serve.

Rice Stuffed Bell Peppers

Serves 4

Prep time: 30 min

Ingredients:

8 bell peppers, cored and seeded

1 cup rice, rinsed

1 onion, finely cut

1 tomato, chopped

1 cup fresh parsley, chopped

3 tbsp olive oil

1 tbsp paprika

Directions:

In a skillet, heat the olive oil and gently sauté the onion for 1-2 minutes until fragrant. Add in paprika and rice and cook for 2-3 minutes more, stirring.

Add the diced tomato and 1/2 cup of hot water. Season with salt and pepper and cook until the water is absorbed.

Stuff each pepper with the mixture using a spoon. Every pepper should be ¾ full. Arrange the peppers in a deep ovenproof dish and top up with warm water to half fill the dish.

Cover and bake for about 20 minutes at 350 F. Uncover and cook for another 5 minutes.

Green Bean and Potato Stew

Serves 5-6

Prep time: 30 min

Ingredients:

1 bag frozen green beans

1 onion, finely cut

4 cloves garlic, crushed

3-4 potatoes, peeled and cut in small chunks

2 carrots, cut

1 tbsp tomato paste, dissolved in 1/2 cup water

4 tbsp olive oil

salt and pepper, to taste

1/2 cup fresh dill, finely cut, to serve

Directions:

In a casserole, gently sauté the onions and garlic in olive oil. Add in green beans and all remaining ingredients.

Cover and simmer over medium heat for about 30 minutes or until all vegetables are tender. Sprinkle with fresh dill and serve.

Cabbage and Rice Stew

Serves 4

Prep time: 30 min

Ingredients:

1 cup long grain white rice

2 cups water

1 small onion, chopped

1 clove garlic, crushed

1/4 head cabbage, cored and shredded

2 tomatoes, diced

1 tbsp paprika

2 tbsp olive oil

1/2 tsp cumin

salt, to taste

black pepper, to taste

1/2 cup parsley, finely cut, to serve

Directions:

Heat the olive oil in a large pot. Add the onion and garlic and cook until transparent. Add in paprika, cumin, rice and water, stir, and bring to a boil.

Simmer for 5 minutes. Add the shredded cabbage, tomatoes, and cook for about 25 minutes, stirring occasionally, until the cabbage cooks down. Season with salt and pepper and serve sprinkled with parsley.

Rice with Leeks and Olives

Serves 4-6

Prep time: 30 min

Ingredients:

6 large leeks, cleaned and sliced into bite sized pieces (about 6-7 cups of sliced leeks)

1 onion, cut

20 black olives pitted, chopped

2 1/2 cup hot water

1/4 cup olive oil

1 cup rice

freshly-ground black pepper, to taste

Directions:

In a large saucepan, sauté the leeks and onion in the olive oil for 4-5 minutes. Cut and add the olives and 1/2 cup water. Bring temperature down, cover saucepan and cook for 10 minutes, stirring occasionally.

Add rice and 2 cups of hot water, bring to boil, cover, and simmer for 15 more minutes, stirring occasionally. Remove from heat and allow to 'sit' for 30 minutes before serving so that the rice can absorb any liquid left.

Paprika Rice

Serves 6-7

Prep time: 30 min

Ingredients:

1 cup rice, rinsed

1 large onion, chopped

2 red peppers, cut

1 can tomatoes, undrained and diced

1 tbsp paprika

3 tbsp olive oil

1 tsp summer savory

½ cup fresh parsley, finely cut

1 tsp sugar

Directions:

In a large saucepan, heat olive oil and gently sauté the onion and peppers for 1-2 minutes until fragrant. Add in paprika and rice and cook, stirring constantly until the rice becomes transparent.

Add in 2 cups of hot water and the canned tomatoes. Stir, and season with salt, pepper, summer savory and a teaspoon of sugar to neutralize the acidic taste of the tomatoes.

Simmer over medium heat for about 20 minutes. When ready sprinkle with parsley and serve.

Roasted Cauliflower

Serves 4

Prep time: 30 min

Ingredients:

1 medium cauliflower, cut into florets

4 garlic cloves, lightly crushed

1 tsp fresh rosemary

salt, to taste

black pepper, to taste

1/4 cup olive oil

Directions:

In a deep bowl, combine olive oil, rosemary, salt, pepper and garlic together. Toss in cauliflower and coat well.

Place in a baking dish in one layer and roast in a preheated to 350 F oven for 20 minutes; stir and bake for 10 minutes more.

Spring Potatoes with Herbs

Serves 4-5

Prep time: 30 min

Ingredients:

2.25 oz small potatoes

5 tbsp olive oil

1 tbsp dried mint

1 tbsp finely chopped parsley

1 tbsp dried rosemary

1 tbsp dried oregano

1 tbsp fresh dill

1 tsp salt

1 tsp black pepper

Directions:

Wash the young potatoes, cut them in halves if too big, and put them in a baking dish.

Pour the olive oil over the potatoes. Season with the herbs, salt and pepper. Bake for 30 minutes at 350 F.

Orzo with Zucchinis

Serves 4-5

Prep time: 20 min

Ingredients:

1 cup orzo

2-3 medium zucchinis, peeled and diced

1/2 onion, finely cut

1/3 cup white wine

3 tbsp olive oil

1 tbsp dried oregano

1/3 cup fresh dill, finely cut

2 tbsp fresh squeezed lemon juice

1 tsp salt

1/2 tsp black pepper

Directions:

Cook the orzo according to package directions and rinse thoroughly with cold water when you strain it. Add in a tbsp of olive oil, stir, and set aside.

Gently sauté the onion and zucchinis in 2 tbsp of olive oil, stirring, until the onion is translucent. Add oregano and white wine and cook, uncovered, on low heat for 10 minutes. Add in orzo and stir to combine well. Stir in lemon juice, dill, and simmer, covered, for 5 more minutes.

Breakfasts and Desserts

Quick Tofu and Vegetable Scramble

Serves: 4

Prep time: 10 min

Ingredients:

2 14-ounce blocks extra-firm tofu, crumbled

1/2 small onion, chopped

1 tomato, diced

1 red pepper, chopped

1 can black beans, rinsed, drained

1/4 cup coarsely chopped fresh cilantro

4 tbsp olive oil

black pepper, to taste

1 1/2 tsp ground turmeric

salt, to taste

Directions:

In a large pan sauté onion over medium heat for 1-2 minutes, stirring. Add in tomatoes and pepper and cook, stirring occasionally, until softened, 3-4 minutes.

Stir in tofu and turmeric. Add beans and cook, stirring often, until heated through, 1-2 minutes. Stir in cilantro, season with salt and pepper and serve.

Season with black pepper and serve.

Raisin Quinoa Breakfast

Serves: 2

Prep time: 20 min

Ingredients:

½ cup quinoa

1 cup water

1 tbsp brown sugar

1 tsp cinnamon

½ tsp vanilla

½ tsp ground flaxseed

2 tbsp walnuts or almonds, chopped

2 tbsp raisins

Directions:

Rinse quinoa and drain. Place water and quinoa into a small saucepan and bring to a boil. Add cinnamon and vanilla. Reduce heat to low and simmer for about 15 minutes stirring often.

When ready, place a portion of the quinoa into a bowl, drizzle with brown sugar and top with flaxseed, raisins and crushed walnuts.

Citrus Quinoa Breakfast

Serves: 2

Prep time: 20 min

Ingredients:

½ cup quinoa

1 cup water

1 orange, peeled, cut into bite-sized pieces

2 tbsp blanched almonds, chopped

2 tbsp cranberries

1 tsp lemon zest

½ tsp vanilla

Directions:

Rinse quinoa and drain. Place water and quinoa into a small saucepan and bring to a boil. Add vanilla and lemon zest.

Reduce heat to low and simmer for about 15 minutes stirring often. When ready, place a portion of the quinoa into a bowl and top with orange segments, cranberries and almonds.

Quinoa Vanilla Pancakes

Serves: 4

Prep time: 15 min

Ingredients:

1 cup cooked quinoa

1/2 cup apple sauce

1/2 tsp baking powder

1/2 tsp salt

1 tbsp sunflower oil

1 tbsp lemon juice

1 tbsp vanilla extract

maple syrup, honey or fruit, to serve

Directions:

Combine all ingredients into a medium bowl.

Heat a nonstick skillet over medium to medium-low heat. Drop batter by heaping tablespoonfuls into the skillet. Allow the pancakes to slowly cook and when the edges are obviously formed flip the pancake.

Serve warm with maple syrup, honey, nut butter or fresh fruit.

Avocado and Olive Paste Toast

Serves: 4

Prep time: 10 min

Ingredients:

1 avocado, peeled and finely chopped

2 tbsp black olive paste

1 tbsp lemon juice

Directions:

Mash avocados with a fork or potato masher until almost smooth. Add the black olive paste and lemon juice. Season with salt and pepper to taste. Stir to combine.

Toast 4 slices of rye bread until golden. Spoon 1/4 of the avocado mixture onto each slice of bread.

Avocado, Lettuce and Tomato Sandwiches

Serves: 2

Prep time: 5 min

Ingredients:

4 slices wholewheat bread

1 tbsp vegan basil pesto

2 large leaves lettuce

1/2 tomato, thinly sliced

1/2 avocado, peeled and sliced

6 slices cucumber

Directions:

Spread pesto on the four slices of bread.

Layer two slices with one lettuce leaf, two slices tomato, two slices avocado and three slices cucumber.

Top with remaining bread slices. Cut the sandwiches in half and serve.

Avocado and Chickpea Sandwiches

Serves: 4

Prep time: 5 min

Ingredients:

4 slices rye bread

1/2 can chickpeas, drained

1 avocado

2-3 green onions, finely chopped

1/2 tomato, thinly sliced

1/3 tsp cumin

salt, to taste

Directions:

Mash the avocado and chickpeas with a fork or potato masher until smooth. Add in green onions, cumin and salt and combine well.

Spread this mixture on the four slices of bread. Top each slice with tomato and serve.

Winter Greens Smoothie

Serves: 2

Prep time: 3 min

Ingredients:

2 broccoli florets, frozen

1½ cup coconut water

½ banana

½ cup pineapple

1 cup fresh spinach

2 kale leaves

Directions:

Combine ingredients in blender and blend until smooth. Enjoy!

Delicious Kale Smoothie

Serves: 2

Prep time: 4 min

Ingredients:

2-3 ice cubes

1½ cup apple juice

3-4 kale leaves

1 apple, cut

1 cup strawberries

½ tsp cloves

Directions:

Combine ingredients in blender and purée until smooth.

Cherry Smoothie

Serves: 2

Prep time: 4 min

Ingredients:

2-3 ice cubes

1½ cup almond or coconut milk

1½ cup pitted and frozen cherries

½ avocado

1 tsp cinnamon

1 tsp chia seeds

Directions:

Combine all ingredients into a blender and process until smooth. Enjoy!

Banana and Coconut Smoothie

Serves: 2

Prep time: 4 min

Ingredients:

1 frozen banana, chopped

1½ cup coconut water

2-3 small broccoli florets

1 tbsp coconut butter

Directions:

Add all ingredients into a blender and blend until the smoothie turns into an even and smooth consistency. Enjoy!

Baked Apples

Serves: 4

Prep time: 30 min

Ingredients:

8 medium sized apples

1/3 cup walnuts, crushed

3/4 cup sugar

3 tbsp raisins, soaked

vanilla, cinnamon according to taste

Directions:

Peel and carefully hollow the apples. Prepare the stuffing by mixing 3/4 cup of sugar, crushed walnuts, raisins and cinnamon.

Stuff the apples and place in an oiled dish, pour over 1-2 tbsp of water and bake for 20 minutes at 350 F. Serve warm.

Amazing Vegan Banana Bread

Serves: 12

Prep time: 30 min

Ingredients:

2 medium bananas, mashed well

1/3 cup brewed black coffee

3 tbsp flaxseed mixed with 6 tablespoons water and stirred well

1 tbsp chia seeds mixed with 2 tbsp water and stirred well

1/2 cup crushed walnuts

1/2 cup olive oil

1/2 cup maple syrup

2 cups white flour

1 tbsp baking powder

1/2 tsp salt

1 tsp cinnamon

1 tsp vanilla extract

Directions:

Combine oil, maple syrup, the mashed bananas, coffee, flaxseed and chia seeds.

Sift the flour, add in salt and baking powder, then gently fold into the wet mixture. Add walnuts, cinnamon and vanilla and stir.

Bake in a preheated to 350 F oven for about 30 minutes, until brown on top and a toothpick comes out clean.

Apple Cake

Serves: 12

Prep time: 30 min

Ingredients:

4-5 medium apples, sliced, cooked and mashed

1 cup walnuts, chopped

1/2 cup apple cider

1/2 cup sunflower oil

3 1/2 cups flour

1 1/2 cups sugar

1 tbsp baking powder

1/2 tsp baking soda

a pinch of salt

1 tsp cinnamon

1 /2 tsp fresh ground cardamom

1/2 tsp ground cloves

Directions:

Combine flour, baking powder, baking soda and salt. In another bowl, mix sugar, vegetable oil and apple cider, until well blended. Add in spices and stir to.

In a smaller bowl, mash the cooked apples. Add them to the other liquid ingredients and mix well.

Add dry ingredients to wet ingredients. Stir until just combined. Add walnuts and stir again.

Spread batter evenly in a lined 9×13″ baking pan. Bake in a

preheated to 350 F oven for 25 minutes. When completely cooled, dust with powdered sugar and cut.

Pumpkin Baked with Dry Fruit

Serves: 5-6

Prep time: 30 min

Ingredients:

1.5 lb pumpkin, cut into medium pieces

1 cup dry fruit (apricots, plums, apples, raisins)

1/2 cup brown sugar

Directions:

Soak the dry fruit in some water, drain and discard the water. Cut the pumpkin in medium cubes.

At the bottom of an ovenproof baking dish arrange a layer of pumpkin pieces, then a layer of dry fruit and then again some pumpkin. Add a little water.

Bake for 25-30 minutes at 350 F until the pumpkin is golden and there is no more water left. When almost ready sprinkle with sugar. Serve warm or cold.

Pumpkin Pastry

Serves: 8

Prep time: 30 min

Ingredients:

14 oz filo pastry

14 oz pumpkin

1 cup walnuts, coarsely chopped

1/2 cup sugar

6 tbsp sunflower oil

1 tbsp cinnamon

1 tsp vanilla

1/3 cup powdered sugar

Directions:

Grate the pumpkin and steam it until tender. Cool and add the walnuts, sugar, cinnamon and vanilla.

Place a few sheets of pastry in the baking dish, sprinkle with oil and spread the filling on top.

Repeat this a few times finishing with a sheet of pastry. Bake for 20 minutes at medium heat. Let the Pumpkin Pie cool down and dust with the powdered sugar.

Apple Pastry

Serves: 8

Prep time: 30 min

Ingredients:

14 filo pastry

5-6 apples, peeled and diced

11/2 cup walnuts, coarsely chopped

2/3 cup sugar

6 tbsp sunflower oil

1 tbsp cinnamon

1/2 tsp vanilla extract

1/3 cup powdered sugar

Directions:

Cut the apples in small pieces and mix with the walnuts, sugar, cinnamon and vanilla.

Place two sheets of pastry in the baking dish, sprinkle with oil and spread the filling on top. Repeat this a few times finishing with a sheet of pastry. Bake for 20 minutes at medium heat. Let the Apple Pastry cool down and dust with the powdered sugar.

Granny's Vegan Cake

Serves: 12

Ingredients:

1/2 cup sugar

1 cup fruit jam

1 cup cool water

1/2 cup vegetable oil

1 cup crushed walnuts

1 tsp baking soda

21/2 cups flour

1 tsp vanilla powder

½ tsp cinnamon

Directions:

Combine the baking soda with the jam and leave for 10 min. Add sugar, water, oil, walnuts and flour in that order.

Mix well and pour in a round 10 x 2-inches cake pan. Bake in a preheated to 350 F oven. When ready turn over a plate and sprinkle with powdered sugar.

FREE BONUS RECIPES: 10 Ridiculously Easy Jam and Jelly Recipes Anyone Can Make

A Different Strawberry Jam

Makes 6-7 11 oz jars

Ingredients:

4 lb fresh small strawberries (stemmed and cleaned)

5 cups sugar

1 cup water

2 tbsp lemon juice or 1 tsp citric acid

Directions:

Mix water and sugar and bring to the boil. Simmer sugar syrup for 5-6 minutes then slowly drop in the cleaned strawberries. Stir and bring to the boil again. Lower heat and simmer, stirring and skimming any foam off the top once or twice.

Drop a small amount of the jam on a plate and wait a minute to see if it has thickened. If it has gelled enough, turn off the heat. If not, keep boiling and test every 5 minutes until ready. Two or three minutes before you remove the jam from the heat, add lemon juice or citric acid and stir well.

Ladle the hot jam in the jars until 1/8-inch from the top. Place the lid on top and flip the jar upside down. Continue until all of the jars are filled and upside down. Allow the jam to cool completely before turning right-side up.

Press on the lid to check and see if it has sealed. If one of the jars lids doesn't pop up- the jar is not sealed–store it in a refrigerator.

Raspberry Jam

Makes 4-5 11 oz jars

Ingredients:

4 cups raspberries

4 cups sugar

1 tsp vanilla extract

1/2 tsp citric acid

Directions:

Gently wash and drain the raspberries. Lightly crush them with a potato masher, food mill or a food processor. Do not puree, it is better to have bits of fruit. Sieve half of the raspberry pulp to remove some of the seeds.

Combine sugar and raspberries in a wide, thick-bottomed pot and bring mixture to a full rolling boil, stirring constantly. Skim any scum or foam that rises to the surface. Boil until the jam sets.

Test by putting a small drop on a cold plate – if the jam is set, it will wrinkle when given a small poke with your finger. Add citric acid, vanilla, and stir.

Simmer for 2-3 minutes more, then ladle into hot jars. Flip upside down or process 10 minutes in boiling water.

Raspberry-Peach Jam

Makes 4-5 11 oz jars

Ingredients:

2 lb peaches

1 1/2 cup raspberries

4 cups sugar

1 tsp citric acid

Directions:

Wash and slice the peaches. Clean the raspberries and combine them with the peaches is a wide, heavy-bottomed saucepan. Cover with sugar and set aside for a few hours or overnight.

Bring the fruit and sugar to a boil over medium heat, stirring occasionally. Remove any foam that rises to the surface.

Boil until the jam sets. Add citric acid and stir. Simmer for 2-3 minutes more, then ladle into hot jars. Flip upside down or process 10 minutes in boiling water.

Blueberry Jam

Makes 4-5 11 oz jars

Ingredients:

4 cups granulated sugar

3 cups blueberries (frozen and thawed or fresh)

3/4 cup honey

2 tbsp lemon juice

1 tsp lemon zest

Directions:

Gently wash and drain the blueberries. Lightly crush them with a potato masher, food mill or a food processor. Add the honey, lemon juice, and lemon zest, then bring to a boil over medium-high heat.

Boil for 10-15 minutes, stirring from time to time. Boil until the jam sets.

Test by putting a small drop on a cold plate – if the jam is set, it will wrinkle when given a small poke with your finger. Skim off any foam, then ladle the jam into jars. Seal, flip upside down or process for 10 minutes in boiling water.

Triple Berry Jam

Makes 4-5 11 oz jars

Ingredients:

1 cup strawberries

1 cup raspberries

2 cups blueberries

4 cups sugar

1 tsp citric acid

Directions:

Mix berries and add sugar. Set aside for a few hours or overnight.

Bring the fruit and sugar to the boil over medium heat, stirring frequently. Remove any foam that rises to the surface. Boil until the jam sets. Add citric acid, salt and stir.

Simmer for 2-3 minutes more, then ladle into hot jars. Flip upside down or process 10 minutes in boiling water.

Red Currant Jelly

Makes 6-7 11 oz jars

Ingredients:

2 lb fresh red currants

1/2 cup water

3 cups sugar

1 tsp citric acid

Directions:

Place the currants into a large pot, and crush with a potato masher or berry crusher. Add in water, and bring to a boil.

Simmer for 10 minutes. Strain the fruit through a jelly or cheese cloth and measure out 4 cups of the juice.

Pour the juice into a large saucepan, and stir in the sugar. Bring to full rolling boil, then simmer for 20-30 minutes, removing any foam that may rise to the surface. When the jelly sets, ladle in hot jars, flip upside down or process in boiling water for 10 minutes.

White Cherry Jam

Makes 3-4 11 oz jars

Ingredients:

2 lb cherries

3 cups sugar

2 cups water

1 tsp citric acid

Directions:

Wash and stone cherries. Combine water and sugar and bring to the boil.

Boil for 5-6 minutes then remove from heat and add cherries. Bring to a rolling boil and cook until set.

Add citric acid, stir and boil 1-2 minutes more.

Ladle in hot jars, flip upside down or process in boiling water for 10 minutes.

Cherry Jam

Makes 3-4 11 oz jars

Ingredients:

2 lb fresh cherries, pitted, halved

4 cups sugar

1/2 cup lemon juice

Directions:

Place the cherries in a large saucepan. Add sugar and set aside for an hour. Add the lemon juice and place over low heat.

Cook, stirring occasionally, for 10 minutes or until the sugar dissolves. Increase heat to high and bring to a rolling boil.

Cook for 5-6 minutes or until jam is set. Remove from heat and ladle hot jam into jars, seal and flip upside down.

Oven Baked Ripe Fig Jam

Makes 3-4 11 oz jars

Ingredients:

2 lb ripe figs

2 cups sugar

1 ½ cups water

2 tbsp lemon juice

Directions:

Arrange the figs in a Dutch oven, if they are very big, cut them in halves. Add sugar and water and stir well. Bake at 350 F for about one and a half hours. Do not stir. You can check the readiness by dropping a drop of the syrup in a cup of cold water – if it falls to the bottom without dissolving, the jam is ready. If the drop dissolves before falling, you can bake it a little longer.

Take out of the oven, add lemon juice and ladle in the warm jars. Place the lids on top and flip the jars upside down. Allow the jam to cool completely before turning right-side up.

If you want to process the jams - place them into a large pot, cover the jars with water by at least 2 inches and bring to a boil. Boil for 10 minutes, remove the jars and sit to cool.

Quince Jam

Makes 5-6 11 oz jars

Ingredients:

4 lb quinces

5 cups sugar

2 cups water

1 tsp lemon zest

3 tbsp lemon juice

Directions:

Combine water and sugar in a deep, thick-bottomed saucepan and bring it to the boil. Simmer, stirring until the sugar has completely dissolved. Rinse the quinces, cut in half, and discard the cores. Grate the quinces, using a cheese grater or a blender to make it faster. Quince flesh tends to darken very quickly, so it is good to do this as fast as possible.

Add the grated quinces to the sugar syrup and cook uncovered, stirring occasionally until the jam turns pink and thickens to desired consistency, about 40 minutes.

Drop a small amount of the jam on a plate and wait a minute to see if it has thickened. If it has gelled enough, turn off the heat. If not, keep boiling and test every 2-3 minutes until ready. Two or three minutes before you remove the jam from the heat, add lemon juice and lemon zest and stir well.

Ladle in hot, sterilized jars and flip upside down.

About the Author

Vesela lives in Bulgaria with her family of six (including the Jack Russell Terrier). Her passion is going green in everyday life and she loves to prepare homemade cosmetic and beauty products for all her family and friends.

Vesela has been publishing her cookbooks for over a year now. If you want to see other healthy family recipes that she has published, together with some natural beauty books, you can check out her <u>Author Page</u> on Amazon.

Made in the USA
San Bernardino, CA
14 April 2017